T. MAN

Being Happy
Activities for Kids
4-12

50
Fun Activities to Encourage
your Child to Make Decision Independently

TABLE OF CONTENTS

INTRODUCTION

Did you know play is a child's universal right recognized by the United Nations (UN)?

But there is a pandemic of physical activity!

Less than a quarter (24%) of kids aged 6 to 17 engage in 60 minutes of daily physical exercise.

Parents and many health experts still believe that kids are inherently very active physically. Young children were frequently referred to as "supercharged dynamos" in exercise-science textbooks in the 1990s when the author began working on the newly growing subject of physical activity and health. The data, however, runs counter to this conventional viewpoint. Recent longitudinal studies in children and public health monitoring of physical activity levels have shown that physical activity diminishes from the time that children enter school and that the reduction lasts through childhood and adolescence.

How can we boost a kid's development through activities?

- They grow strong muscles, bones, and joints.
- Their muscular control, strength, and coordination will all increase.
- Their heart and lungs will grow into healthy organs.
- They will keep their weight at a healthy level.
- Their posture and balance will both get better.
- Their body will become flexible.
- Chronic illnesses like type 2 diabetes and heart disease are less likely to affect them.
- Their brain will form important connections that will enhance their ability to concentrate and think clearly.

These are just the basic benefits of activities, but play is rarely associated with learning, even though many parents instinctively understand the value of play in children's development.

Most people define learning as mastering a certain new ability, like memorizing counting, the alphabet, writing, etc. They frequently think that playing is merely for enjoyment and that no real learning occurs. However, research indicates that playing is learning. Children gain knowledge via play. Play is a vital part of early childhood education since play-based learning is crucial to a child's development.

Here's how activities encourage mental growth. Activities boost critical thinking abilities, memory, the understanding of cause and effect, and the exploration of the world and one's place in it.

Through activities, young children learn how things fit together. It enables kids to engage their senses and fosters curiosity and exploration, which are the abilities that underpin intellectual growth and cognitive processing.

Children are encouraged to pretend, create, and imagine through activities. Children may conceive, brainstorm, and practice critical thinking abilities via imaginative, open-ended play.

Fun activities are essential for social development since they teach kids how to connect with others, which is another benefit of play. Children learn about social norms and expectations via play, which also gives them a chance to communicate, listen, and come to compromises.

Activities also aid youngsters in understanding and managing their emotions. Children use play to process their feelings and new ideas. For instance, a youngster learns to cope with despair, rage, and grief when they lose a game. Playing also promotes confidence-building and the growth of a person's individuality and self-esteem.

This book is full of exciting and fun activities. The inspiration behind this book is to improve children's physical and mental skills while boosting their happiness and self-awareness. The first chapter of the book briefly dives into the reasons how kids learn the most when they are having fun. The next three chapters include worksheets and activities. The second chapter deals with emotions, thoughts and behavior. The next chapter focuses on getting along with others and making friends. The last chapter hovers over the concept of mindfulness.

I am a child psychologist with more than seven years of experience working with little minds to boost their potential through thrilling and fun activities. I have worked with hundreds of children to regulate their behavior and boost their

LET'S HAVE SOME FUN NOW!

CHAPTER 1:

IS THAT DOPAMINE, THE SECRET TO GROWTH?

Playing games, solving puzzles, and reading books are just a few enjoyable ways to learn new concepts. The enjoyable instruction offers several viewpoints for resolving issues and encourages learners to think creatively. Additionally, it instils traits like perseverance, self-control, and goal-setting. Children may develop imaginative thinking by exploring their curiosity through hands-on experimentation with various materials. Parents need to be aware of the many advantages that enjoyable learning offers. Play, both unstructured and organized, is crucial for a child's development for the following reasons:

- **Play Promotes Cognitive Development**

  What does it mean to "promote cognitive growth"? It implies that play is essential for the development of a healthy brain. Children create their own play while they are not bound by structured play. Activities or timetables directed by adults do not limit them. Unstructured play improves a child's brain's healthy growth. The brain's neural connections are strengthened and boosted by it. We employ these neural connections in the brain during thinking processes.

Unstructured play is also beneficial for developing and preserving the prefrontal cortex. This region affects how a youngster learns, handles challenges, and learns about their surroundings.

- **Play Develops Imagination and Creativity**

    Children use their imaginations when playing. They create imaginary games and get immersed in made-up worlds. Children who figure out numerous solutions gain confidence. They make their own rules and try following them or changing them as needed. They are practical skills for managing life and interacting with others.

    The capacity to see one item as yet another is known as pretend play. For instance, a bucket, a stick, and pinecones can be imagined as a pot, cooking tool, and tasty food. Playing pretend is crucial to a child's healthy growth. It helps kids develop the abilities they'll need for problem-solving and future learning. Additionally, it enhances creativity, which helps people succeed in many aspects of their lives.

- **Play Has Positive Effects on Emotions and Behavior**

    Adults tend to withdraw into calming pursuits when they are feeling overburdened. We exercise, play board games, tend to the garden, go around the block, or sing karaoke with friends. These pursuits are not only diversionary. They allow us to reconnect with the things in life that give us a sense of purpose and bring play back to our lives.

    The only difference is that kids require a lot more playing. It is frequently and regularly can lessen irritation, tension, and worry. It also fosters self-confidence and happiness.

PARENTS CAN HELP LABEL THEIR CHILD'S EMOTIONS BY WATCHING THEM PLAY. "IT SEEMS LIKE YOU ARE ANXIOUS TO GO TO SCHOOL THE NEXT DAY," FOR INSTANCE. CHILDREN CAN TELL THAT ADULTS CARE WHEN THEY LISTEN AND MAKE INQUIRIES. IT CONVEYS THAT THEIR THOUGHTS AND FEELINGS ARE SIGNIFICANT.

Play is a great way to learn. Children learn how to navigate the environment via play so they can understand and process. They investigate group dynamics, sharing, negotiating, dispute resolution, and stand up for themselves.

- **Greater Independence is Encouraged via Play**

Children frequently lack control or input into their everyday activities. They are instructed on when to do it, what to do, and where to be for a large chunk of their days. They can establish the rules and exercise authority in the domain of play. Adults who listen to them and follow their instructions might be the leaders.

Learning to play with others is just as vital as playing independently. Children benefit from having a greater feeling of freedom. Children who are at ease playing alone feel more capable of taking on other duties and finding out their place in the group. Even future group socialization benefits from developing these abilities. Children who are playing alone can pick up social clues by watching how groups interact.

Children can explore their own imaginations and ideas while playing alone. Children's minds take up the challenge when they are alone or even just bored. They come up with innovative and fun ways to keep themselves engaged. "The monotony and seclusion of a tranquil life encourage the creative imagination," Albert Einstein once stated.

- ## Play Enhances Literacy

Language acquisition is a natural trait in children. They develop literacy and language abilities via play and interaction starting in infancy. Babies and toddlers acquire new words when people explain what they hear, see, and do. Syllables and beats are related in poetry and music. Children gain knowledge of the sounds by words and improve their listening abilities as a result.

Children learn about communication via play. Even though they are unable to communicate, they get to practice speaking back and forth! Sharing stories from books aids their understanding of themselves and their part in the society, whether verbally or via pretend play. Stories also show students how language functions and how to organize narratives.

Games and toys are also beneficial. Playing with little toys aids in hand muscle development. This aids writing. Playing "I Spy" and other concentration games improves your ability to observe and pay attention. These abilities improve practicing comprehension by helping kids in understanding context and making connections.

Kids still need to play when they start school. Research shows pupils pay closer attention to their assignments after an unscheduled play break. Play increases curiosity, and boosts learning.

- **Play Improves Physical Fitness**

   Children's bodies are programmed to be active. Physical play, which includes all forms of play that keep kids moving, is something that they require a lot of. It helps them develop their body awareness and fortifies neural connections. It is a terrific sort of activity that motivates kids to be active and healthy.

   All throughout a child's life, the normal energetic play has beneficial and extensive benefits on their health. Physical activity benefits kids regardless of their talents, interests, or opportunities by helping them grow stronger muscles, better bone density, better balance, quicker reflexes, improved motor skills, improved movement control, and improved cardiovascular function, all while having fun!

   Time spent outside each day is essential. It helps youngsters have better mental health and self-control. Put kids in layers and outdoor clothing regardless of the weather so they can enjoy their time outdoors. They will return happier and more at ease inside.

I hope you understand how physical activities help children. I have included thrilling worksheets in this book, too, that will contribute to your child's development. Kids like filling out worksheets; for them, it is just like playing. What could be more enjoyable than ensuring children subtly learn while having fun? The youngsters find worksheets engaging since they require a lot of coloring and planning. They would choose to work on a worksheet over their own textbooks on purpose.

Worksheets are now a fun and effective way to teach children moral principles. They discover them to be intriguing, captivating, and stimulating. When opposed to textbooks, your child will joyfully participate in a worksheet, as you would personally find as a parent. These worksheets also make sure that parents and kids spend quality time together.

CHAPTER 2:

LITTLE BRAINS, BIG FEELINGS

Can you imagine life without thought? For a human, it would not be much of an existence. Thoughts constantly come to mind, whether informative, dull, hilarious, or strange. Unquestionably, thinking is something that comes naturally to us. As flight and swimming are to animals like eagles and dolphins, thinking is to people.

However, comprehending the nature of cognition is much different from just thinking. Like dolphins swim without understanding fluid mechanics and eagles fly without knowing aerodynamics, the majority of us do not completely understand the nature of the mind. Thoughts on cognition as a whole are far less common than thoughts about thinking in general.

Mental cognitions or thoughts are our ideas, viewpoints, and beliefs about who we are and the world around us. They include the perspectives we bring to every situation and encounter that cloud our judgment (for better, worse, or neutral).

An example of persistent thinking is attitude. Repetition and reinforcement of thoughts lead to the development of attitudes.

If you are aware of your attitudes and thoughts, you can manage them.

Our thoughts cause feelings, and those feelings affect how we behave. Let's examine a simple example. The idea of going to a pool makes me happy even though I enjoy being outside near water and swimming. These ideas and feelings will spur me to plan swimming-related events. On the other hand, if the thought of being near water terrifies my friend, she would not go swimming. The same event (swimming) is seen differently by each of us (thoughts), which causes various emotions (pleasure or terror), which causes varied responses (going to the pool or not). We are neither right nor wrong. Simply put, we disagree on what we deem to be enjoyable.

The relationship between your ideas, emotions, and behavior is illustrated here.

Situation: A kid makes a hurtful remark to you at school.

<u>One possible thought</u>

This is my fault. The other kid wouldn't be so mean to me if I were more fun.

→

- Frowning and crying
- Feeling tired
- Paying attention to things you don't like about yourself
- Wanting to be alone

→

I think I am feeling sad.

<u>Another possible thought</u>

This isn't my fault. The other kid just likes making people feel bad.

→

- Clenching fists
- Fast heart beat
- Paying attention to things that you don't like about the other kid
- Wanting to be alone

→

I think I am feeling angry.

2.1
FUN ACTIVITIES

Children who have the ability to manage their emotions, thoughts, behavior, and motor activities are better able to handle a variety of situations. The ability to maintain an adequate degree of arousal in any given circumstance is what we mean when we talk about self-regulation. In addition, self-regulation includes the capacity to produce appropriate behavioral and sensory reactions to input in various contexts and daily activities, as well as the ability to demonstrate self-control, which includes the ability to watch over and manage actions, focus, emotions, motor output, and social interactions.

Self-regulation abilities can include a kid being calm and problem-solving, asking an adult for advice or assistance when another child takes his toy or being able to self-regulate, manage their impulses, and maintain their volume of voice in a quiet environment like a library. A youngster exercising self-control in a classroom or school could be able to pay attention and remain seated while the instructor is speaking, or he might be able to stick with his class and walk in line in the corridor.

Children need to be able to handle feelings and events and develop appropriate reactions throughout the day. Children must learn to manage their desires so that they can quit doing something if necessary and engage in something even if they do not want to. Children may gain the required skills to self-regulate while having fun by playing games that teach self-control!

ACTIVITY: THE FREEZE DANCE

With a small group of children or family members, have a dance party and instruct everyone to keep still when the music is turned off. The first mover is disqualified from continuing to the next round. The final dancer standing wins.

ACTIVITY: PARACHUTE!

Who does not enjoy parachute games? A non-competitive social connection enables kids to regulate their movements, listen, and recall instructions. This activity screams self-control and following directions. Give pupils a chance to decide their own course of action by throwing little balls towards the center of the parachute. The top balls should bounce when the parachute is shaken, but not so much that the balls fly out.

ACTIVITY: BALLOON TAP

Balloons and a large area are all you need for this entertaining game. Place pupils in a circle and divide them into two teams in alternating order (one kid is team 1, the next kid is team 2, the next kid is team 1, and so forth). Balloons should be arranged in a circle. Call "Team 1" now! Team 1 members alone should tap the balloons. Only kids on Team 2 should tap the balloons after switching to Team 2. Continue turning it on every 20-30 seconds. Kids will have to pay close attention to hear the aural signal indicating their team's time to tap.

Want to involve everybody in the fun? Make use of colorful balloons. No one should tap any balloons that are that color after you call out the "off-limits color." and then alter the color! Kids will need to pay attention to the aural trigger and control their urges when the forbidden hue is nearby.

ACTIVITY: BODY MIX

The leader will call out various body parts for the kids to touch in the game "Body Part Mix Up." For instance, when the teacher yells "knees," the kids touch their knees. Make one rule, to begin with. Touch your toes each time the leader says, "Head," rather than your head. The kids must pause, consider their behaviors, and refrain from just reacting in order to do this. Knees, head, elbow! The leader yells. The kids' toes, elbows, and knees should all be touched. To modify bodily parts, keep practicing and adding new rules.

ACTIVITY: DRAW IT OUT

Making a collage or having children sketch a picture of the various emotions they experience is a creative and engaging technique to help children name their feelings. You can ask questions such as, "How does it feel when you're happy?" or "What does it look like when you are feeling angry?" Encourage your children to use any items they choose and be as inventive as possible.

ACTIVITY: TRAFFIC LIGHT GAME

It takes practice to learn to control all that joyful energy. The traffic light game is a wonderful exercise for learning to stop and slow down. This also applies to children that run ahead.

Draw circles in green, yellow, and red. Learn to move quickly on the green, more slowly on the yellow, and stop completely on the red. When my 5-year-old goes too far ahead of me, I still say, "Red light means stop," because the humor of it helps when nothing else does.

ACTIVITY: ASSIGN EMOTIONS A COLOR

The capacity to recognize emotions is essential. The use of this color wheel will help kids identify their emotions by associating them with certain colors. If children are aware of how emotions feel, they can begin to acquire coping skills.

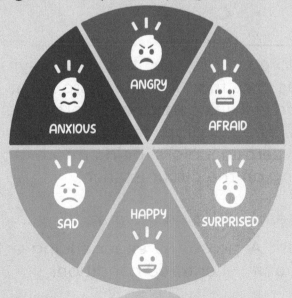

ACTIVITY: EMOTIONAL TWISTER

Putting certain body parts on various colored dots on a mat in the classic game of Twister may be a great way to raise emotional awareness while keeping the exercise entertaining and lively. The mat, the spinner that directs which body parts to move, some little pieces of paper, and a writing implement are all you need.

You will list a distinct situation where certain emotions and actions would be necessary on each sheet of paper. While you aim to stay as far away from the red zone as you can, a yellow zone could be more bearable in some circumstances.

You can include any of the following environments on the pieces of paper:

- School
- Homework Time
- Sports Field
- Lunchtime
- Airport
- A friend's house
- Restaurant
- Library
- Cinemas
- Car

The many colored dots on the map symbolize various emotional states that function like a stoplight for traffic. This stoplight method will link particular colors to various emotional intensity states. These colors relate to numerous aspects of daily life, with certain colors being more appropriate than others depending on the circumstance.

The purpose of each color on the mat:

- **Green:** A person is experiencing a tranquil, joyful, and emotionally-centered condition.

• **Yellow:** This color serves as a warning of elevated feelings and heightened awareness. In these phases, children are still in control of their emotions, but they are more likely to be feeling tension, anxiety, silliness, or enthusiasm. When concentration and silence are not necessary, these feelings could be more suited.

• **Red:** A person is experiencing tremendous emotions, which, given the circumstances, might be extremely disruptive or inappropriate. Feelings of fury and anger mainly characterize this emotional zone.

• **Blue:** Recharge opportunities or non-emotionally charged moments. This could show up as boredom, a lack of enthusiasm, or disinterest. This category is typically used to group emotions that are characterized as depressed or sad.

For 2-3 players, it is best to let people get twisted while playing.

ACTIVITY: ORCHESTRA

Give children percussion instruments to tap and wave, and instruct them to follow a front-row child who is acting as a conductor and holding a baton (a pen, ruler, or stick will do). Everyone must adjust their pace and calm down by the conductor's prescribed tempo. Children will learn to coordinate their body motions to produce a pleasing sound.

ACTIVITY: COLOR RUN

Tell the kids that they will be moving about the room. Depending on the color of the paper you are holding up, they are to move. The yellow paper indicates a regular walking rate, whereas the blue paper indicates a sluggish pace. They stop if you hold out a red piece of paper. Try out various locomotor activities, such as marching, leaping, and stationary running.

ACTIVITY: BREATHING EXERCISES

Exercises involving breathing are among the most powerful techniques for calming and centering oneself, which is why they play such a significant role in emotional regulation. Our breathing is shallower and faster when we are worried, nervous, or furious.

You may teach youngsters some simple breathing techniques to assist them in controlling their emotions. They're a terrific technique to swiftly defuse a stressful situation. De-escalating an emotionally charged scenario can be as simple as pausing and taking a few deep breaths. The most well-known breathing techniques include balloon, belly, and bunny breathing.

Here is how you can perform the bunny breath:

Just do three fast sniffs through the nose and one thorough exhalation. Invite children to play the role of rabbits smelling the air in search of other bunnies, safety or tasty carrots. When used in this way, it makes for a nice cleaning breath. It may also be used to aid children who are really distressed and unable to breathe since it will enable them to connect to their exhale and allow them to breathe rather than spinning out.

ACTIVITY: CONTROL PANEL GAME

I started referring to my son's core self as his "control panel" since he is so fascinated by technology and robots. He controls his control panel, I said, and he has the ability to alter his mood or his conduct.

The next time he got angry, he declared, "I want to hit something!" Your control panel is malfunctioning, I remarked. How can we turn it on again? After giving it some thought, he said, "I can turn my furious switch!!!"

It worked. He turned on his deep breathing switch and turned off his crazy switch. We discussed what had enraged him.

Easter egg hunts do not have to be reserved only for special occasions. Preparing the plastic eggs and concealing them both take some preparation for this exercise. The enjoyment in this game comes from locating the eggs and using emotional control abilities to solve problems. For this game, you will need a couple of baskets or containers, some plastic eggs, and a permanent marker.

Each egg will have a distinct emotion-filled face painted on it. On the egg tops, draw various eyes and facial expressions; on the bottom, draw various mouths. Ask the participants to locate the eggs and identify the emotion displayed on each one.

Once they have decided on an emotion, instruct them to place it in a container that matches the colors and symbolism of the stoplights.

IT IS TIME FOR WORKSHEETS. YAY!

INTERESTING WORKSHEETS

Do you want to help your kids understand, embrace, and work through their powerful feelings? These worksheets can be used to assist kids in exploring, tracking, and understanding the effects of their actions.

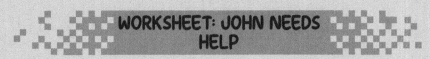
Hello young people! Here is the first worksheet. John's first day at a new school has come. He is experiencing anxiety as a result of his negative ideas. Can you assist him in replacing his negative ideas with good ones?

NEGATIVE THOUGHTS

I do not have any friends here. No one is going to like me!

My friends at my old school are having fun without me.

I'm so nervous. The kids will probably think I am weird.

The school is SO big. I know for sure that I am going to get lost!

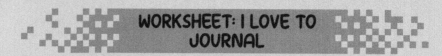

WORKSHEET: I LOVE TO JOURNAL

You need to fill out this form with your daily behavior decisions and the next day's improvement plans. Let's go.

MY BEHAVIOR JOURNAL

DID I REACH MY BEHAVIOR GOALS FROM YESTERDAY?

☐ YES (AWESOME JOB)

☐ NO   WHAT KEPT ME FROM REACHING MY GOALS?

_____

GOOD BEHAVIOR THAT I DISPLAYED TODAY:

_____

_____

POOR CHOICES THAT I MADE TODAY:

_____

_____

HOW DID THESE CHOICES AFFECT MYSELF AND OTHERS?

_____

_____

MY BEHAVIOR GOALS FOR TOMORROW:

_____

_____

WHAT DO I NEED TO DO TO REACH THESE GOALS?

_____

_____

You can use this worksheet to find a solution for your current state of emotions. Let's go step-by-step.

HOW TO WORK THROUGH YOUR EMOTIONS?

NAME THE EMOTION

- I am feeling _____

  Examples: Angry, Sad, Stressed
- I feel like _____

  (Describe the feeling in a few words)

IDENTIFY THE CAUSE

- I Was _____ *(where)*
- I remember noticing _____

CHALLENGE THE EMOTION

- *Was my _____ (feeling) appropriate to the situation?*
- *Is this situation a distress that I can control?*
- *If it is out of my control, is this a distress I have to accept and tolerate?*

IDENTIFY THE BEHAVIOR

- *When I felt _____ I _____ (behavior, action)*
- *What I wish I had done was _____ .*

Solve this exercise for any complex scenario troubling you.

What Happened?

Feeling

Thought

Behavior

Do you know what emotions look like on your face?

MY FEELING FACES

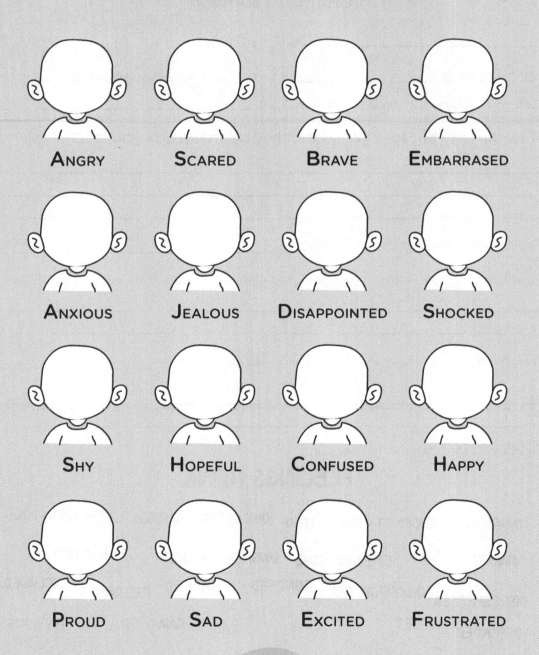

ANGRY

SCARED

BRAVE

EMBARRASED

ANXIOUS

JEALOUS

DISAPPOINTED

SHOCKED

SHY

HOPEFUL

CONFUSED

HAPPY

PROUD

SAD

EXCITED

FRUSTRATED

This worksheet provides instructions that encourage you to express your feelings to others.

FEELING EXPRESSION PROMPT

Use this worksheet to help you express your feelings to someone!

_____(their name).

I am feeling_____. *(Are there any other feelings you are experiencing? Use the feelings blanks to help you identify more feelings! _____ _____)*

I feel this way because (What did they do that made you feel this way?)

_____ _____

_____ _____

_____ _____ .

I have been feeling this way since _____ .

I wanted to let you know how I feel because *(why did you want to share your feelings with them?)*

_____ _____

_____ _____ .

I am hoping that *(what do you want to happen after they hear your feelings?)* _____

_____

_____

Thank you for listening to me!

FEELINGS BANK

UNHAPPY   SHOCKED FRUSTRATED   DISGUSTED   SCARED   MISUNDERSTOOD

ANGRY   HURT   EMBARRASSED   UNSAFE   SAD   INSULTED

DISRESPECTED   DISAPPOINTED   ANNOYED   ASHAMED   BETRAYED   EXCLUDED

OFFENDED   UPSET   ANNOYED   ANXIOUS

The focus of this worksheet is behavior comprehension.
Detective, hurry up and get to work!

BEHAVIOR REFLECTIONS

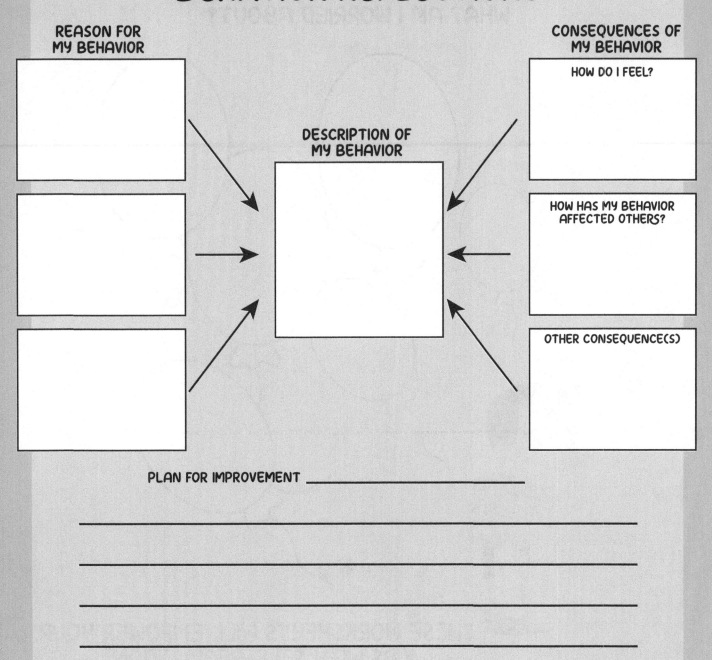

**REASON FOR
MY BEHAVIOR**

**DESCRIPTION OF
MY BEHAVIOR**

**CONSEQUENCES OF
MY BEHAVIOR**

HOW DO I FEEL?

HOW HAS MY BEHAVIOR
AFFECTED OTHERS?

OTHER CONSEQUENCE(S)

PLAN FOR IMPROVEMENT _____

_____

_____

_____

_____

This worksheet will assist in identifying your worries since, as we all know, stress and anxiety may cause you to become mentally uncontrollable. After that, you may let go of your concern balloon and watch them go off.

WHAT AM I WORRIED ABOUT?

THESE WORKSHEETS WILL EMPOWER YOUR KIDS WITH SELF-REGULATION.

CHAPTER 3:
MAKING FRIENDS

A big part of getting along with others and making friends is perspective-taking. An essential life skill is an ability to perceive and comprehend the world from another person's perspective. Find out the value of perspective-taking and how you may encourage kids to acquire it.

Every person sees the world from a different viewpoint. Two individuals or 200 people can experience an identical incident, and their reactions may differ greatly. Why is it crucial that we comprehend another person's viewpoint?

We do not exist in solitude, and in order to succeed or complete any task, each individual must interact with and collaborate with others. It is of utmost importance that we are able to engage in perspective-taking in order to deal with others effectively. To cooperate, communicate, and demonstrate empathy and understanding, we must comprehend how others view the world. As an adult, it is expected of you to respect the thoughts and experiences of others by listening to them. It is essential for friendships, professional and sexual relationships, and all connections in general.

Taking perspectives requires a variety of specific abilities, such as:

- **Figuring Out Another Person's Emotions:** We must apply our knowledge and comprehension of someone while putting aside our beliefs, views, and sentiments to try to grasp how they must be feeling or thinking.

- **Inhibiting Command:** We must put our own ideas on wait to view the world from someone else's perspective. We put our own desires on hold in order to think about someone else when we exercise self-control to engage in perspectivetaking.

- **Flexible Thinking:** We need to think differently than we often do in order to change our viewpoint. This calls for cognitive flexibility to enable us to shift our attention away from ourselves and toward someone else.

Social competence requires children to improve empathy, understanding and perspective taking.

In this chapter, I will help your little one develop the skills they need to boost their social competence and make friends through worksheets and activities. It will help them make friends at school too.

3.1

FUN ACTIVITIES

How can we support kids in learning social skills, which include the capacity to understand emotions, work with others, form friendships, and resolve disputes? Children learn from our behavior as role models and gain from our efforts to foster situations that value restraint. However, nothing beats actual practice. Children require hands-on practice with taking turns, teamwork, self-regulation, and understanding different perspectives in order to learn and flourish.

HERE ARE SOME EFFECTIVE SOCIAL SKILLS EXERCISES FOR ALL KIDS OF AGE THAT ARE BASED ON RESEARCH.

ACTIVITY: THE MATCHING GAME

Each youngster receives a marble, and their task is to locate the other children who have the same color marble. As soon as all of the groups are finished, they join arms and remain together. This is a wonderful method to bring kids from diverse backgrounds together and to reinforce the concept that individuals from different backgrounds may share interests. Additionally, it helps young children practice naming different colors.

ACTIVITY: TURN-TAKING

Babies and young children can make sudden actions of compassion, although they might be wary of strangers. So how can we impart the concept of a buddy to them?

One effective technique is to have the youngster perform reciprocal, lighthearted acts of kindness with a stranger. For instance, the youngster can roll a ball backward and forward or alternately push a toy's button. It's possible for the youngster and the stranger to exchange intriguing things.

The youngsters appeared to flick a switch when psychologists tested this straightforward strategy on 1-2-year-olds.

The infants started to see their new play-buddies as persons they could share with and help. However, if kids just played with a stranger without any reciprocity, there was no such impact.

ACTIVITY: YOUNG CHILDREN'S RHYTHM AND MUSIC-MAKING GAMES

Kids have a natural tendency to want to help others. How can we support this inclination? According to research, music-making and group singing is excellent social skills exercises for promoting supportive, cooperative behavior.

For instance, think about this game.

When The Frogs Wake Up

First, you gather a group of unfamiliar children and have them focus on a "pond" made up of a blue colored blanket laid out on the ground with many "lily pads" drawn on it. On the lily pads are toy frogs.

The kids are then informed that the frogs are asleep. We must assist the frogs in waking up this morning. Give the kids some basic musical instruments and help them sing a wake-up song as they round the pond in rhythm to the music.

Following the game with 4 years old kids, the researchers evaluated the youngsters' natural desire to assist other kids. Children who "awakened the animal, frog" with the musical exercise were more inclined to assist a classmate who was having difficulty than those who did not.

ACTIVITY: IMAGINATIVE, THEATRICAL GROUP GAMES

Kids need to be able to control their emotions when something distressing occurs if they want to develop social competence. They must learn to maintain their composure. Moreover, playing dramatic pretend with others is a promising approach for children to enhance these abilities.

To attempt this strategy, include kids in cooperative pretend play activities such as dressing up as a family of animals, taking turns turning yourself into statues or pretending to make a dish together as chefs.

ACTIVITY: CHECKER STACK

A game for maintaining two-way communication is the checker stack. Some children find it challenging to carry on a discussion with classmates. The game Checker Stack, necessitates that players take speaking turns and do not go off-topic

A set of tokens that can be stacked, such as poker chips or checkers, plus a friends group or an adult to assess the value of each player's efforts are all you need to play this two-player game.

The game starts when Player One lays out a token and says something to open a dialogue. After making an acceptable comment, Player Two adds another checkmark on top of the original one.

The players continue the dialogue, each in turn. How much longer can they handle it? How much higher can their stack go? The flow of the conversation is disrupted, and the player loses when they say something off-topic or irrelevant, which ends the game.

ACTIVITY: TEAM BUILDING

Team building is a type of play that encourages coordination. Children must coordinate, bargain, and communicate when they use blocks to build anything together. Do these social skill-building exercises have an impact?

It makes sense intuitively, and there is research to back it, that children who require more support to develop their social communication skills might benefit from a specific cooperative building therapy program called "LEGO®-based therapy" (Owens et al., 2008). Researchers have decided that this therapy is a "promising treatment" for boosting social connections with children on the ASD spectrum after reviewing published studies (Narzisi et al., 2020).

ACTIVITY: PLAYING COOPERATIVELY

Cooperative games come in a variety of formats. Some, like the numerous board games currently on the market, are more sedentary. Others are energetic or physical, such as William

Haskell's "Timeball" and "Islands" which were tried on more advanced primary school pupils (2004.)

A study shows that researchers discovered that participating in these games for 12 weeks caused a slight but discernible improvement in "prosocial" conduct, which is being helpful and kind to others (2004.)

"Timeball"

Kids run out in an open area and play this game while standing with their feet together. A ball is presented to one youngster. After giving the ball to another youngster, the first child sits down. The other kid repeats the technique until all the children are sitting.

Children must toss the ball carefully since the game's goal is to help everyone be seated as fast as possible and because the ball cannot hit the ground. In addition, students should think about how tough it will be for other children on following rounds while determining where to pass the ball next: If youngsters pass the ball in a method that make some kids so much far away making it difficult to throw the ball and miss a catch— the team will lose. Kids will thus probably want to talk about strategies.

"Islands"

Hula hoops—one for every three students—and a group of young toddlers are required to play "Islands." Afterwards, you put the hoops on the ground and let the children play nearby. Every youngster must enter a hoop when you whistle, and each hoop must hold three or more children. To fit within a hoop, kids will need to work together and hold onto one another.

ACTIVITY: CONVERSATIONS ABOUT EMOTION BASED ON STORIES

These social skills may be done pretty much anywhere: Children should be given an emotional story to read and then encouraged to discuss it.

What made the main character furious? What types of things aggravate you? What do you do to defuse tension? Children who participate in group discussions on emotion consider their own experiences and gain knowledge about the variety of responses that others have to their environment. And that comprehension could aid children in honing their "mind-reading" skills.

Participants outperformed their counterparts in a control group after two months, demonstrating a considerable increase in their comprehension of emotion. Additionally, they performed better on tests of empathy and "theory of mind," or the capacity to consider the ideas and views of others (2014.)

ACTIVITY: NEIGHBORHOOD GARDENING

It sounds obvious that group gardening may help youngsters develop social skills, and research proves the concept, but I haven't seen any thorough trials on the topic.

Children that participate in community or school gardening are likely to have better social skills.

What activities may kids engage in in the garden? Let me tell you how sixth graders were engaged in group gardening in a recent research. The children were divided into groups. Each group was tasked with caring for a certain garden bed. Children were also asked to undertake soil tests, identify various plants, note plant development, and observe snails (2021.)

THESE ACTIVITIES WILL HELP YOUR CHILD LEARN SOCIAL COMPETENCE SKILLS. LET'S MOVE ON TO WORKSHEETS.

3.2

INTERESTING WORKSHEETS

Socially competent children are better able to comprehend who they are, how to interact with others, and how the world works. Kids that are socially adept are very wellrounded. They like to have new experiences, make friends and get along well with others. These youngsters are well-mannered in social situations.

This worksheet will help you figure out the difference between appropriate and inappropriate responses.

		Appropriate Behavior	Inappropriate Behavior
	I cannot figure something out	I ask for help	I break my pencil
	An adult gets upset with me.		
	I accidently break something.		
	I lose a game.		
	I do not get what I want.		
	I feel left out.		
	I drop something and make a mess.		
	I make a mistake.		
	My schedule changes.		

Use the boxes below to draw examples of when you showed good and poor social skills.

MY SOCIAL SKILLS

HAVING GOOD SOCIAL SKILLS MEANS YOU BEHAVE IN A WAY THAT MAKES PEOPLE ENJOY BEING AROUND YOU.

HAVING POOR SOCIAL SKILLS MEANS THAT YOUR BEHAVIORS MAKE OTHERS NOT WANT TO BE AROUND YOU.

GOOD

POOR

How would you keep the conversation going?

You won't believe the kind of day that I'm having!

I'm really not looking forward to tomorrow.

It sure is a real nice day outside!

I feel like everyone is ignoring me today.

I can't wait to go to the movies this weekend!

I feel really sad. You probably wouldn't understand

This worksheet will help you understand how to give people compliments, as it is an important social skill.

Complimenting People You Know:

Compliments for this person you know: _____

Compliment something they own

Compliment what they did

Their **clothes, jewelry, watch**

Something you know *about them*

Their **hairstyle, haircut**

What **they said**

45

What are good manners?
Can you tell me the difference
between good and bad manners?

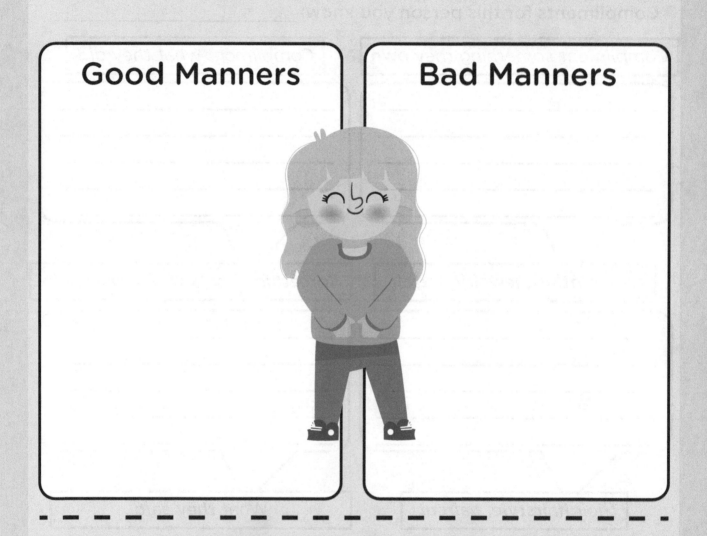

Good Manners

Bad Manners

Saying please and thankyou	Sneezing on someone	Cutting in line
Letting others go first	Interrupting	Taking Turns

WORKSHEET: WHAT DO YOU SAY?

This worksheet will help you improve your talking skills! It will also help you be more kind to others.

Elephant and piggie have some challenges. Look at the pictures below. Write what they could say to help each other.

1 Elephant cannot dance.

_____
_____

Elephant thinks that elephants cannot dance. What could Piggie say?

2

_____
_____
_____

Piggie want to play the trumpet, but it doesn't sound right. What could elephant say?

3

_____
_____
_____

Elephant dropped his ice cream! What could Piggie say?

4

_____
_____

Piggie want to play outside, but it's raining. What could Elephant say?

This worksheet will help you introduce your own self to people around you.

SELF-INTRODUCTION

Worksheets for Kids

COULD YOU HELP ANNIE INTRODUCE HERSELF TO MIKE?

This worksheet will help you act right when your friend is not feeling good.

Can I show empathy?

Write or draw how you would show empathy to how a friend is feeling.

When a friend is sad, I can...

When a friend is angry, I can...

When a friend is nervous, I can...

When a friend is disappointed, I can...

When a friend is lonely, I can...

When a friend is confused, I can...

When a friend is unwell, I can...

49

We should not say all the things we think in our heads. This worksheet will help you realize what things are not nice to say. Here are some examples.

Filter the Thoughts Activity

FILTER
IT

SAY IT

I'm going to hit you!

NO! Me First!

NO! I won't do it!

I wish he was dead!

I'm disappointed!

This is hard!

I'm angry!

I'm worried!

I need some help!

I need a break!

Filter the Thoughts

SAY IT

FILTER IT

I HOPE YOU ENJOYED THESE WORKSHEETS!

CHAPTER 4:

MINDFUL LIVING

Paying attention to your present and what is going on in the now is mindfulness.

Being mindful involves paying attention to your body and what you see, hear, smell, and taste. You could even experience emotions physically, like a tightness or positive sensation.

Being mindful includes being aware of what your mind is doing.

What occurs when you begin to become aware of these experiences?

By paying close attention to your surroundings, you may concentrate more intently and enhance many aspects of your life. This increased sensitivity to your own senses will advantage you in many aspects of your life.

You can perform better in sports, academics, or music with improved attention. You'll do better on tests as a result of it. We usually do better when we have the capacity to focus on what we are doing, right?

STILL, THERE'S MORE.

When you are unhappy, angry, or annoyed, paying attention to your surroundings might assist you in calming down. You may be joyful and feel good with mindfulness, and it also helps you deal with difficult emotions.

DO YOU WANT TO TRY IT? I WOULD DO IT!

THAT IS A FANTASTIC TECHNIQUE TO INTRODUCE MINDFULNESS TO YOUNG CHILDREN.

Your youngster will get more in touch with their emotions and ideas with mindfulness activities. Less emotional reactivity and a better capacity to listen and communicate more effectively come with greater self-awareness of their feelings. It will allow them to make sound decision making.

FUN ACTIVITIES

Even for very young kids, the world is becoming increasingly hectic and sometimes seems overwhelming. Our mental health benefits from standing back from this hustle and establishing tranquil, introspective areas in our life.

Young children who practice mindfulness lead more balanced lives. When children practice mindfulness, their thoughts focus on the here and now, and they develop more emotional awareness. Parents may assist their kids to live more present-focused lives and be more thankful by modelling mindful living for them.

ACTIVITY: MAKE BUBBLES

Children adore bubbles! Encourage your children to inhale carefully, and then let out a calm exhale into the bubble wand. Encourage them to picture their worried thoughts as a bubble that will eventually explode in the air as it flies away. The youngsters' concerns vanish when the bubble vanishes. This activity is a fantastic approach to introduce your children to mindful breathing, which can assist them in calming down more rapidly under pressure.

Bubble-blowing is another meditative hobby. It helps kids to forget their worries and concentrate on blowing bubbles. Want to test them and sharpen their focus? Let's see who can blow the largest bubble! As they make try after attempt, watch them light up.

ACTIVITY: TEDDY BREATHING

Teach your kids how to breathe slowly and consciously. Place a plush animal on their chest while they lie on the ground. Tell them to take a few deep breaths and see their stuffy rise before exhaling and watching it descend. Check out what happens if you breathe more quickly, more slowly, or hold your breath.

ACTIVITY: PRACTICE COSMIC YOGA

Yoga, which mixes breathing, posture, and stretching, is said to have existed for more than 5,000 years! While you're spending more time indoors, it may keep you active and healthy while also promoting calm.

Cosmic yoga is a lot of fun! It's vibrant and upbeat, and the instructor frequently dons outrageous costumes!

There are many options to pick from, ranging from Star Wars to Frozen, as classes are frequently themed after literature, TV shows, and movies.

ACTIVITY: MAKE A LISTENING GROUP

Visit a nearby park or nature reserve with a small group of kids. Ask the kids to listen out for various noises as you sit in a circle. Ask kids to raise their hands when they wish to share a sound they can hear rather than yelling out.

ACTIVITY: MINDFUL POSING

Body postures are a simple method for kids to start practicing mindfulness. Inform your children that striking amusing positions may make them feel courageous, powerful, and pleased to get them thrilled.

Send the youngsters to a calm, recognizable location where they may feel secure. Then, request that they attempt this pose:

> The Superman position is performed by standing with the feet slightly wider than the hips, the fists clenched, and the arms extended as high as possible.

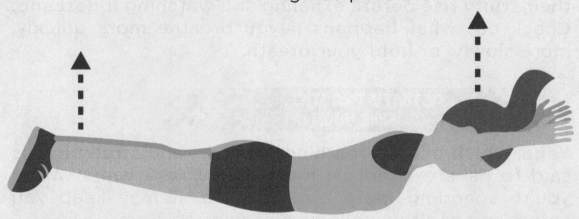

After a few repetitions of either of these stances, ask the children how they feel. You might be shocked.

ACTIVITY: USE YOUR SENSES

Use your senses to teach your children how to be present in the now. They are forced to focus on their immediate surroundings during this traditional mindfulness activity, which helps them forget their troubles. One minute spent concentrating on each sensation helps calm rushing, tense thoughts.

Kids must glance around and ask themselves the following questions as they go through the 5 senses exercise:
What can I see?

- What sound do I hear?
- What fragrance is there?
- How do I feel?
- What can I taste?

Introduce them to items and even things they may not have ever heard, seen, smelled, or touched. Give them the prop and instruct them to describe it using their senses thoroughly. Is the item soft or rough? How hefty or light is it? Is it odorous?

ACTIVITY: TRACING FINGERS

Kids should silently sit down and extend one hand in front of them with the palm facing in. Show them how to draw the contour of their hand from the base of the thumb up, around the thumb, and around each finger. Ask them to take a breath while they trace upward. Exhale as they go downward.

ACTIVITY: MAKE A WISH LIST

Even though we're spending more time indoors and away from our friends and loved ones, we still daydream about all the amazing things we'll do once we're permitted to go outside once more. Why not compile a wish list of everything you want to accomplish? Get a pen and paper, and make a list of everything you want to do, along with the people you would like to do it with—from friends to relatives. To get you started, consider writing down the following:

Attending birthday parties, having picnics, swimming, going to the library, and playing in the park are all enjoyable activities.

ACTIVITY: SAFARI

The Safari activity is a fantastic approach to teaching youngsters mindfulness. With this game, a routine stroll becomes a brand-new, exhilarating adventure.

Assert that you are going on a safari, and your children's task is to spot as many birds, insects, creepy crawlies, and other creatures as they can. It will be especially important for younger children to concentrate on all of their senses in order to discover anything that walks, swims, crawls, or flies (2017).

The mindfulness walk is a comparable adult activity. Children respond to this activity in the same way that adults respond to a mindful walk: they become more aware and present.

ACTIVITY: DRAW IT OUT

One of the most enjoyable mindfulness exercises for children is drawing. Tell your children to close their eyes and focus on positive thoughts. Give them a notepad and some crayons when they've made a decision, then instruct them to sketch it.

Ask them to consider how it feels to hold the crayon as they are sketching. Next, instruct them to concentrate on the paper's texture. Ask them to explain the colors they used to create the image. Directing their entire attention to the process of painting will help the children's nervous thoughts.

As your kid draws, encourage them to speak aloud about their creations. Additionally, you'll see that people could become sidetracked and chatter while drawing. When this occurs, politely request a description of their actions. What are you currently doing? Which portion are you currently drawing?

ACTIVITY: TEXTURE BAG

Put various items in a bag with various forms and textures. Encourage the kids to feel each thing with their hands before explaining it as well as they can to the other kids without allowing them to see it.

ACTIVITY: TAKE FOUR SQUARE BREATHS

For older kids, this activity is a helpful tool. Take a four-count inhalation. Hold your breath for four counts. Count to four as you exhale. Hold your breath for four counts. Repeat a few times, then resume your regular breathing.

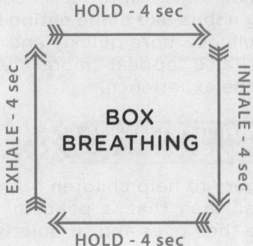

HOLD - 4 sec

EXHALE - 4 sec

INHALE - 4 sec

BOX
BREATHING

HOLD - 4 sec

ACTIVITY: BUILD MANDALAS

A mandala is a circular pattern with recurring hues, forms, and patterns that radiate outward from its center. Use this adaptable, imaginative tool to enhance your practice of mindfulness. You may use various things from your house or the outdoors to construct a 3D mandala or draw a circle on the paper and add patterns and repetition to it. For a quick method to interact, mandala coloring pages are also available for download.

ACTIVITY: MINDFUL EATING

Give your children a nutritious snack, such as an apple or a granola bar, to practice mindful eating. Ask them to take time to examine the delightful food, paying particular attention to its shape and color, before they consume it. Ask them to describe the sensation of the food in their hands. Tell them to reflect on the treat's flavor and texture once they have finished their mouthful.

Several advantages come from mindful eating. Studies demonstrate that this approach can help avoid unhealthy eating habits like binge eating by enabling the body to sense fullness more quickly and reduce anxiety. Snacking might also appear more delightful if you concentrate on the experience.

ACTIVITY: ATTEMPT GUIDED IMAGERY

Use guided imagery to help children refocus their active thoughts. Pick an area that is peaceful and unbroken. Ask kids to close their eyes and sit quietly. Slowly read a guided imagery script as calming music is playing in the background.

ACTIVITY: SQUISH UP!

Feeling perplexed, incensed, or depressed over circumstances beyond your control is acceptable. Something soft and squishy may be really relaxing to play with in your hands. You may use a variety of squishy materials, such as play dough, cloud dough, and bread dough. Our favorite is bread dough since you can use it to later create a beautiful loaf of handmade bread.

The dough must first be "kneaded" in order to create a flawlessly fluffy loaf of bread. This entails rolling the dough using the palm of your hand on a flat surface, flipping the dough over, and repeating the procedure. You may also enjoy yourself by tossing, whacking, and pounding the dough. Enjoy!

ACTIVITY: OBSERVE CLOUDS

Watch the weather for this exercise since you want a strong wind and perhaps partial cloud cover. Get the kids outside to lie down and gaze up at the clouds. As you travel, ask them to keep an eye out for forms and note how the clouds change.

ACTIVITY: CREATE CUSTOM STRESS BALLS

In addition to being entertaining, this activity provides your children with a fantastic mindfulness tool. Take a funnel and place it in the neck of some colored balloons. Pour the chosen filling in slowly with the assistance of your children. For bouncy stress balls, use cornstarch, flour, or sand. For a more solid texture and a less messy experience, you may alternatively add dried rice or birdseed.

Once the balloons are full, tie them up and let the youngsters paint or attach stickers on the exterior. Kids may physically release any unwanted sentiments by simply squeezing stress balls. They are also excellent for use as a meditation focus.

ACTIVITY: JUST LISTEN

Have kids close their eyes and sit quietly. To help children concentrate on hearing what is going on around them, ask them to calm their minds. Set a one-minute timer. They could hear the chirping of birds outside, the humming sound of the radiator, or their own breathing. Encourage them to refrain from thinking while they are listening. Have them open their eyes when the timer goes off. Ask them how they feel physically and mentally compared to before the exercise.

ACTIVITY: CREATE A GRATITUDE FLOWER

Watch the weather for this exercise since you want a strong wind and perhaps partial cloud cover. Get the kids outside to lie down and gaze up at the clouds. As you travel, ask them to keep an eye out for forms and note how the clouds change.

According to scientists, gratitude may improve our mental health in a variety of ways, including by promoting better sleep and more self-assurance. We may become appreciative of what we have when faced with difficult circumstances, such as being away from friends and spending less time outside.

Hey kids, by creating a thanks flower, you may express your emotions creatively. Create a large flower by either sketching one out on paper or creating a collage flower out of colored paper scraps. List one item you are grateful for on each of the lovely petals. Invite your entire family to participate so you can compare the notes you made.

The following are some suggestions that you might wish to use:

- Your home
- Hugs
- Phone
- Toys
- Chocolate
- Music
- Calls with Friends

These activities will help your child interact with others with mindful behavior. Let's get onto worksheets.

INTERESTING WORKSHEETS

Kids may gain a lot from practicing focusing and concentration skills involved in mindfulness in a variety of ways. Their capacity for sustained focus is improved. It aids them in comprehending and controlling their emotions, promotes overall wellness and stress management, and facilitates the development of a relationship with nature.

Moreover, they benefit from having a greater awareness of their senses and bodies and develop empathy and compassion for others.

SO SHOULD WE BEGIN?

This worksheet will help you think about happy things with mindfulness.

I am happy when... _____

_____

_____

I am grateful for... _____

_____

_____

I am excited for... _____

_____

_____

I am relaxed when... _____

_____

_____

I am good at... _____

_____

_____

A good deed I have done recently is... _____

_____

_____

The good deed I will do next is... _____

_____

_____

If I am sad or upset I will... _____

_____

_____

WORKSHEET: MAKING USE OF YOUR SENSES

This worksheet will help you calm down by using your five senses.

I can see...

I can hear...

I can smell...

I can taste...

I can touch...

This worksheet is about items of different textures and how they feel. Write up some words associated with the texture too. Examples of items include rocks, leaves, pillows, walls etc.

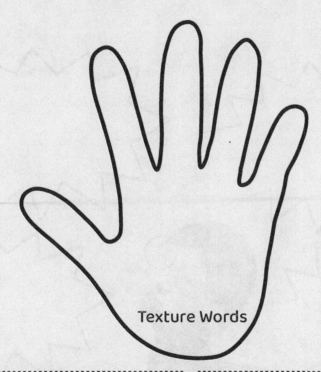

Texture Words

How does it feel?	What is the item?
1. _____	1. _____
2. _____	2. _____
3. _____	3. _____
4. _____	4. _____
5. _____	5. _____
6. _____	6. _____
7. _____	7. _____
8. _____	8. _____
9. _____	9. _____
10. _____	10. _____

This worksheet will help you rise above your anxiety and respond mindfully.

Analyze your day with mindfulness.

Rose

A highlight, a success, or something positive that happened.

Bud

New ideas or something you're looking forward to knowing or understanding more.

Thorn

A challenge you experienced, or something you can use more support with.

- What was a highlight today?
- How have you been successful?
- What are you most proud of?

- What are you looking forward to?
- Describe opportunities for learning that excite you.
- What needs growth and nurturing?

- What are you looking forward to?
- Describe opportunities for learning that excite you.
- What made it hard to be successful?

Look up the numbers and their associated colors to fill this picture up.

I WISH YOU A MINDFUL LIFE!

A FINAL WORD

A pleasant, healthy childhood might prepare your children for success in adulthood. However, many parents are curious about how to raise content children in the modern environment. Giving your children temporary pleasure or instant gratification won't make them happy. In actuality, the reverse is true.

Give them a skill set that enables them to experience long-term happiness through adulthood. They can forgo immediate satisfaction in order to accomplish their objectives. By forming wholesome, lifelong habits, you may aid in your children's development of these abilities.

Never undervalue the influence of outdoor play. Children benefit from playing outside, climbing trees, swinging, and digging in the soil. According to studies, natural aromas like mowed grass, lavender, and pine trees help improve your child's happiness. To help your child feel happier right away, you may urge them to read a book outside or complete their homework on the porch.

Moreover, kids may experience brief pleasure from running away from homework to play with friends, eating an extra cookie, and watching TV for hours rather than finishing their responsibilities. Although, low self-control ultimately does more harm than good. According to a 2014 research, those with higher self-control express more positive moods.

However, it is interesting to notice that those with higher self-control avoided temptation more frequently than others. In a sense, they prepared themselves to be content.

Begin instilling self-discipline in your child at an early age. You could help her in achieving this in a number of ways.

Place a basket for cell phones in the kitchen. To prevent her from being tempted to browse the internet while completing her homework, advise your kid to place her smartphone in the basket while she is working on it.

Before going to bed, place all digital devices in a designated area of the home. Thus, while your kid is in bed, she will not feel the temptation to use her tablet or phone.

Stock up on nutritious food options in the cabinets and fridge. If you have sweets around the home, make it harder for guests to get to them by keeping them on shelves or hidden in the pantry back.

THIS BOOK WILL KEEP YOUR CHILDREN HAPPY AND CONTENT WHILE BOOSTING THEIR MENTAL AND PHYSICAL HEALTH. IF YOU HAVE LIKED THIS BOOK, PLEASE LEAVE A REVIEW ON AMAZON.

Made in the USA
Las Vegas, NV
21 October 2023

79466982R00044